The Animal Kingdom:
Science Themes for Primary Children

Teacher Manual

Dr. Kathryn T. Hegeman, Ed.D.

Royal Fireworks Press
Unionville, New York

Royal Fireworks Press
P.O. Box 399
41 First Avenue
Unionville, NY 10988-0399
(845) 726-4444
fax: (845) 726-3824
email: mail@rfwp.com
website: rfwp.com

ISBN: 978-0-89824-031-3

Printed and bound in Unionville, New York, on acid-free paper using
vegetable-based inks at the Royal Fireworks facility.

Publisher: Dr. T.M. Kemnitz
Editor: Jennifer Ault
Book and cover designer: Christopher Tice

7jly17

Table of Contents

Chapter One

Introduction

The Theme: A Plan for Teaching Children in the Primary Grades

A thematic approach to teaching provides teachers with a long-range plan that interrelates subjects and gives children opportunities for practice in many areas of skills development. In addition, it allows teachers to accommodate children's different ability levels, learning styles, and interest areas.

The animal kingdom is a theme whose major content focus is drawn from the life sciences: biology, ecology, and environmental studies. Most children enjoy learning about animals, and their enjoyment can be used to encourage them to explore and investigate nature and the animal kingdom. The activities in the student book are fused with the language arts and furnish extended opportunities for children to develop understanding and to broaden concepts.

The materials presented in this book enable teachers to capitalize on their students' enthusiasm by providing creative ideas for learning activities that put science concepts to work while sharpening skills. The activities enable students to work independently, with a partner, or in small groups. Children learn how to attack problems with confidence and to take pleasure in skill mastery and in doing well. They also come to understand and appreciate the beauty and bounty of nature.

Modular Organization

The Animal Kingdom is divided into ten independent but related learning modules—one for each month of the school year. Each module is a relatively self-contained unit; they can be taught separately or in a sequence. A modular approach that is not interdependent is not only practical to organize but has several other advantages:

- Children can succeed in each module, regardless of prior experience (i.e., entering into the class later in the year or being sick does not penalize a child).

- Each module allows children to learn, practice, and expand skills at different levels of proficiency.

- The relatively few modules covered allow for a more in-depth approach that encourages investigation of topics.

- These investigations allow children to use thinking processes, research skills, and study skills in order to develop science concepts and become independent learners.

Each module introduces a different animal and explores its adaptations to the environment. There is a passage about the animal to read aloud to the children. The questions that follow the passages should motivate the children to learn more about the animals and their habitats. The children are encouraged to recall, summarize, and explain what they have learned.

A Planning Sheet is included for each unit. This format allows for flexibility in planning which skills are to be taught and which materials and resources are to be used. The Planning Sheet aids teachers in designing learning experiences that will enable children to apply concepts and discover more about natural phenomena.

Chapter Three of this book contains information that teachers can use to help them plan the modular lessons. This information uses Bloom's Taxonomy as a basis for structuring learning opportunities for children that will include struggling students as well as children ready to engage in higher-order thinking tasks. It provides many helpful examples; teachers are encouraged to use these as springboards to creating their own questions and activities.

Learning by Doing: Process Skills Development

In order to solve problems and develop science concepts, children need to learn how to use a number of specific process skills. These skills enable them to learn how to evaluate and interpret information and reach a logical conclusion. The children can then share what they have learned with confidence. Some important process skills are:

FINDING INFORMATION

Observing
Researching
Recording

USING INFORMATION

Measuring
Classifying
Comparing and contrasting
Validating

SHARING INFORMATION

Communicating

Skills mastery helps children achieve cognitive growth. Both content and process are important if children are to assimilate knowledge and become independent learners. Children's self-concepts are enhanced by developing independence as learners: seeking information, working on problems, and sharing the results of their efforts.

Planning Sheet

Module: _____

Concepts: _____

_____

_____

_____

Vocabulary: _____

_____

_____

Questions to stimulate thought and discussion:

Remembering _____

_____

Understanding _____

_____

Applying _____

_____

Analyzing _____

_____

Evaluating _____

_____

Creating _____

_____

Planning Sheet

Knowledge Objectives: _____

_____

_____

Skill Objectives: _____

_____

_____

Related Subjects: _____

_____

_____

Activities: _____

_____

_____

_____

Resources and Materials: _____

_____

_____

_____

Values and Attitudes: _____

_____

Evaluation: _____

_____

Planning a Learning Center

Animals generally are highly appealing to young children, and multiple resources about animals are readily available. The teacher's task is not only to provide these multiple resources but to be aware of their value, purpose, and intent. Children need access to learning materials, but they also need the freedom to use those materials if they are to develop skills of self-management and self-direction.

A practical first step for teachers who want to develop self-management skills in their students is to involve the children in the planning of the unit by developing a learning web. This is a good way to organize thoughts, ideas, and questions into appropriate learning activities. This web need not be completed at once but may be augmented as the students' needs, abilities, and interests suggest new directions for learning.

As the children complete the learning web, they learn classifying and outlining skills. As an added bonus, the web can serve as a point of reference for evaluation, review, and reinforcement of concepts.

The degree of the children's involvement in planning learning activities will vary according to their level of maturity. The process may take several days, depending on the ability of the group to sustain involvement. Use the following simple steps:

1. List the topic on a large whiteboard.

2. Encourage the children to brainstorm and call out ideas related to the topic. Record their ideas.

3. Plan a learning web by grouping related ideas.

4. Work with the children to develop a list of questions.

5. Use the learning web and questions based on Bloom's Taxonomy (see Chapter Three of this book) to help plan learning activities at different levels.

6. Develop a list of resources, materials, experts, and fieldtrips. Encourage suggestions from the children.

7. Have the children select topics they wish to explore.

8. Plan for sharing and evaluation.

Planning with the children gives them direction and purpose, fosters goal-oriented behavior, and develops oral expression. They learn to express their thoughts and respect the ideas of others.

The activities suggested by the learning web can be incorporated within the framework of a learning center. This flexible approach encourages peer interaction and accommodates a wide range of abilities. Learning center experiences encourage children to relate ideas and try things out for themselves.

Learning centers vary in structure and form and can be readily adapted to many types of classrooms. However, planning a learning center that meets divergent student needs involves more than assembling a random assortment of clever, theme-related activities to keep children occupied. The goals of a learning center are to:

- Provide a wide variety of materials and resources at different ability levels
- Promote open-ended, student-selected activities
- Encourage process-oriented (as opposed to product-oriented) education
- Expand the knowledge that children assimilate, and extend concepts related to the theme
- Improve and expand thinking and learning skills
- Extend opportunities to engage in problem-solving experiences
- Foster social development by encouraging positive habits and attitudes
- Provide opportunities for product development, sharing, and evaluation by the children

Keep the learning center simple. Avoid the excessive use of elaborate and often distracting decorations. Whenever possible, use real objects and accurate reproductions.

Learning Centers

• Provide a framework for theme activities
 	
• Provide for different levels of learning
  • below level
  • at level
  • above level
	• Provide subject knowledge
	
	• Provide for skills development
	
	• Provide for enrichment outside the bounds of the regular curriculum
	  • teach
	  • reinforce
	  • enrich
		• Utilize different learning modalities
		
		• Review facts
		
		• Extend learning and concepts
		
		• Develop vocabulary
		
		• Encourage independent study
		
		• Promote special interests
		  • data research
		  • data organization
		  • data sharing

Every learning center needs six things to make it work:

1. Teacher attention (i.e., relevance to classroom work)
2. Suitable materials and resources
3. Rules for center use
4. Specific directions for activities
5. Children engaged in cooperative learning with one another
6. Recognition and use of children's products

THE ANIMAL KINGDOM
LEARNING CENTER

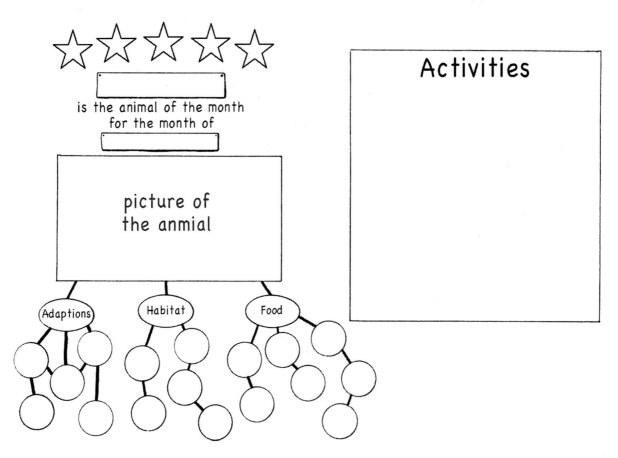

☆ ☆ ☆ ☆ ☆

is the animal of the month
for the month of

picture of
the anmial

Adaptions   Habitat   Food

Activities

Chapter Two
Overall Theme Plan:
The Animal Kingdom

Theme: The Animal Kingdom

The Animal Kingdom is a thematic unit for children in kindergarten through the third grade. It is specifically designed to develop concepts and expand vocabulary. Activities provide opportunities for creative behavior. These experiences encourage children in the primary grades to develop higher-level thinking skills. Children become independent learners as they expand their study skills and engage in problem-solving exercises.

Module: Animal of the Month

The student book features a different animal each month. Children of all ability levels are intrigued by animals and are curious about nature. Discovering the animal kingdom motivates and holds inquisitive young children's interest.

Modular Units

Whale
Cat
Deer
Horse
Lion
Elephant
Kangaroo
Robin
Ladybug
Turtle

General Concept

In every environment, animals have certain problems, but they have special ways of overcoming those problems. These special ways are called adaptations. Animals live in water environments or land environments because they are adapted to life in those environments.

Knowledge Objectives

Throughout each unit, children acquire information and understanding. They develop concepts and expand their vocabulary. Learning is structured to promote higher-level thinking skills and problem-solving abilities. The objectives of *The Animal Kingdom* include:

1. To identify what zoologists, ornithologists, and veterinarians do

2. To understand the difference between vertebrates and invertebrates and to be able to give examples of each

3. To be able to identify and discuss the problems of life in land environments

4. To be able to identify and discuss the problems of life in water environments

5. To be able to identify the kind of environment each animal studied normally inhabits

6. To be able to state how each animal's adaptations suit it to live in a certain environment

7. To know the adaptations of various animals in order to compare and contrast them

8. To be able to classify animals according to the types of food they eat (omnivores, herbivores, carnivores)

9. To be able to explain how an animal's adaptations help it obtain food

10. To be able to explain how an animal's adaptations provide protection from danger

11. To be able to explain how an animal's adaptations affect locomotion

12. To be able to explain how an animal's adaptations enable it to hibernate

13. To be able to classify animals as predator or prey

14. To be able to explain how some animals are adapted to live both on land and in water

15. To be able to explain how animals are interdependent and interact with other living organisms in the environment

16. To be able to explain the common needs of animals: food, water, air, and warmth

17. To understand that aquatic mammals have the same needs for air as do land mammals

18. To understand the concept of a life cycle

19. To understand that the stages of the life cycle vary with different animals

20. To understand that each stage in the life cycle may have many different adaptations

21. To understand that all animals reproduce

22. To be able to identify some of the differences between methods of reproduction and their effect on stages of the life cycle

23. To understand that humans must play a part in protecting animals and the natural environment

Skills Development

Children learn to use a number of specific skills as they work through each module. They:

1. Observe carefully using all their senses, study, and think about what they see (e.g., explore a natural habitat and acquire information)

2. Read to answer questions and acquire information

3. Gather information from pictures, photographs, and charts

4. Gather and retain facts from listening to information sources (readings, recordings, etc.)

5. Develop an ability in oral language through questions, brainstorming, and group discussion

6. Develop record-keeping skills by writing and other means, such as photos and drawings

7. Recognize and are able to name the various animals and their physical characteristics

8. Recognize different animal characteristics as adaptations for survival

9. Recognize and are able to classify a variety of environmental and animal sounds

10. Recognize a variety of plant and animal life in each of several habitats

11. Learn how to plan and outline a flow chart to guide study activities

12. Select and choose appropriate resources for learning activities

13. Practice using specific tools, measuring devices, equipment, and other materials to obtain information and develop projects

14. Develop library, study, and research skills

15. Develop an awareness of animals in our cultural heritage (both in fact and fantasy) through literature, nursery rhymes, poetry, and other sources

16. Apply math and other subject area skills (e.g., maps, social studies) for use in charts, graphs, or recording devices to explain animal growth and behavior

17. Learn about organizations interested in preserving wildlife

18. Expand writing and research skills by writing to wildlife agencies and environmental organizations

19. Learn how to classify, group, and code information about animals and related topics

20. Learn how to compare and contrast animals and related topics

21. Validate information through problem solving and investigations

22. Compile information necessary to complete projects

23. Participate in discussions, planning, and work projects in a cooperative manner

24. Assume responsibility for maintaining materials, projects, work space, and equipment in good order

Values and Attitudes

The learning activities in *The Animal Kingdom* will promote children's self-reliance and skills mastery. These are necessary elements for children to experience joy in learning. Gains in self-concept will enable youngsters to cope with a variety of emotional, social, and intellectual demands. In addition, helping children discover the wonder of natural phenomena will help to instill a respect and reverence for all life.

Evaluation

Teachers should evaluate the children on an individual basis for concepts learned, skills mastered, and social growth. This can be accomplished through observations and informal tests. Student performance in various activities can also be evaluated and recorded by the teacher.

Whale

2

Animal Kingdom Planning Sheet

Animal of the month:

Whale

Month:

My Activities Plan

_____
_____
_____
_____
_____

Some things I want to know about:

Food

_____
_____

Habitat

_____
_____

Adaptations

_____
_____

Habitat

The _____ is home to the whale.

Draw some things found in this habitat.
Draw the animal too.

Can you include other animals that might live here?

4

Animal Record Sheet

Animal's Name: Whale

Draw the animal.

Now label the animal's parts.

Record of important facts:

1. _____
2. _____
3. _____
4. _____
5. _____
6. _____

Special words: _____

_____

Animal's habitat: _____

5

Animal Facts: Whale

Passage to Read Aloud

If you wanted to find the biggest animal in the world, where would you look? You would look in the ocean. The blue whale is larger than any other animal, and it lives in the ocean. The place where an animal lives is called its *habitat*. Who has seen a whale? It is hard to imagine just how big a blue whale is without ever seeing one. It is about 100 feet long, which is about as long as two semi trucks lined up in a row. The blue whale can weigh as much as 150 tons, or more than twenty elephants.

These huge animals never leave the water. Whales are well-adapted to their life in the ocean. They have a fish-like form. They have front flippers and a flat tail to propel them through the water. Yet they are not fish. Whales are warm-blooded creatures. They are mammals. Mother whales have live babies and feed them milk.

Whales have a layer of thick fat under their skin called blubber. This helps them keep warm in the cold polar oceans. This is called *adaptation*. They breathe air like people. Most whales travel close to the surface and come up every fifteen minutes or so to breathe. Fish have gills for breathing. Whales have lungs. They breathe through blow holes on top of their heads. The whale's spout is a stream of air and water being squirted out of the hole on top of its huge head.

There are different kinds and sizes of whales. Some whales have teeth and are called toothed whales (*odontocetes*). Sperm whales, killer whales, and porpoises belong to this group. Whales that don't have teeth are called baleen whales (*mystecetes*). The blue whale is a baleen whale, so it doesn't have teeth. Instead, it has a strainer of whale bone that hangs down inside its mouth. This traps small fish and plants called plankton. It also keeps out larger fish that might get caught in the whale's throat. Some other baleen whales are humpbacks, grays, and fintails.

The whale has small eyes but good vision. Its eyes are well suited to life in the ocean. A whale's ears are no more than tiny holes in the side of its head, but whales' hearing is very good. Whales make gnashing noises with their mouths. Then they listen with their keen ears for the echoes to bounce back from things in their path. This is called *sonar*. This is especially helpful to toothed whales who hunt squid deep in the ocean where it is very dark.

Whales live and travel in family groups. When winter comes to the Arctic and Antarctic Oceans, whales travel many thousands of miles to places where the ocean is warm. As they cruise along, they make great dives and leaps in the water. They communicate and warn one another of danger using whistles, groans, squeaks, and other shrill sounds that can be heard for many miles.

Whales have their babies in the warm waters. The father whales are called bulls. The mothers are called cows. A cow has a calf every other year. She is pregnant for ten to twelve months. Baby whale calves are born tail first so they will not drown. Once the calf is out of her body, the cow quickly pushes her baby to the surface so it can breathe. The calf cannot suck, so the cow squirts milk into her baby's mouth. Soon the babies grow larger. Then the whales start on their long trip back to the cold polar oceans where food is plentiful.

In the past, whales were valuable to people. Whales were used to make soap, perfume, and animal foods. People have hunted and killed many whales. Today there aren't many whales left. We must be careful, or someday they will be extinct.

QUESTIONS:

1. Can you describe a whale?

2. How does a whale's keen hearing help it find food?

3. How do you know that a whale is a mammal?

4. If you were a baby whale, what would your life be like?

5. Which of a whale's adaptations to life in the ocean do you think is most important for its survival?

Whale Planning Sheet

Module: _____

Concepts: _____

_____

_____

_____

Vocabulary: _____

_____

_____

Questions to stimulate thought and discussion:

Remembering _____

_____

Understanding _____

_____

Applying _____

_____

Analyzing _____

_____

Evaluating _____

_____

Creating _____

_____

Whale Planning Sheet

Knowledge Objectives: _____

_____

_____

Skill Objectives: _____

_____

_____

Related Subjects: _____

_____

_____

Activities: _____

_____

_____

_____

Resources and Materials: _____

_____

_____

_____

Values and Attitudes: _____

_____

Evaluation: _____

_____

Cat

6

Animal Kingdom Planning Sheet

Animal of the month:

Cat

Month:

My Activities Plan

_____

_____

_____

_____

_____

Some things I want to know about:

Food

_____

_____

Habitat

_____

_____

Adaptations

_____

_____

The Cat Family Portrait

A baby cat is called a _____.

8

Animal Record Sheet

Animal's Name: Cat

Draw the animal.

Now label the animal's parts.

Record of important facts:

1. _____

2. _____

3. _____

4. _____

5. _____

6. _____

Special words: _____

_____

Animal's habitat: _____

9

Animal Facts: Cat

Passage to Read Aloud

What animal is small, furry, has four legs and a tail, bright eyes and keen ears, sharp teeth, eats meat, and is usually a family pet? You might guess either a dog or cat. Dogs and cats are the most common pets in the United States today. But if the words "it purrs" were added, you'd know it was a cat. Everyone is familiar with the cat's purr of contentment and pleasure, as well as the familiar meow. Both dogs and cats are carnivores. They eat meat. Both dogs and cats usually have five claws on their front feet and four on their hind feet. Can you name some other ways cats and dogs are alike and some ways they are different?

Cats are much-loved members of many households. If well taken care of, a cat will live happily with a family for many years. Some cats can live seventeen or more years. Cats come in many breeds and color varieties. Most of these belong to two groups: short-haired and long-haired. A Persian cat is a long-haired, and a Siamese is a short-haired.

How do families decide which pet to choose? Some people naturally prefer the graceful, curious, and independent cat. Others may think a cat is more practical for their family's needs. Cats do not object to being left alone for long periods of time. If you are at school and your parents are at work most of the day, a cat is a good choice for a pet. It does not need to be walked. It can use a litter box. The cat makes a good pet for a city family.

Have you ever seen a cat licking itself? The cat is working hard at staying clean. From the time a kitten is old enough to sit up, it begins to wash itself. It is natural for a cat to want to be clean.

Kittens weigh only about a quarter of a pound at birth and usually come in litters of two to five. They depend completely on their mother for milk for the first month. Kittens must be with their mothers for at least six weeks. After that they can be weaned. Kittens are considered full grown at eight months and are called cats. It is a good idea to take kittens to a veterinarian so they can get shots to protect them from diseases.

Cats have relatives that live in the wild. A cat's family name is *felis catus*. Some members of the family are the African lion, the Bengal tiger, and the leopard. These beautiful animals are disappearing from their natural habitat. Some zoos are trying to breed these large cats in captivity.

Like their wild relatives, cats hunt at night. A cat's eyes can make use of all possible light at night. A cat's whiskers help it to feel its way in the dark. A cat uses its excellent hearing to listen for sounds that humans often cannot hear. When it senses a mouse nearby, the cat crouches. Then it stalks it with its body close to the ground. It crouches low with whiskers spread and ears turned forward. It then pounces on its prey with extended claws and catches the mouse.

Many cats are affectionate and purr when stroked. They are playful. Cats like simple toys such as yarn or a rolled-up piece of paper. Cats are comfort-loving animals. They spend much of their time sleeping. They like to find sunny spots to take naps. They also like to rest on high places such as windowsills. Above all else, cats are curious. An open door or box or paper bag invites them to poke and explore.

19

Cat communicate in many ways besides meowing or purring. They use their tail, eyes, ears, or whiskers to express many moods such as anger, fright, or contentment.

A kitten that is cared for well and shown love grows into a cat that is an affectionate family member.

QUESTIONS:

1. Have you ever seen a newborn kitten?

2. Can you describe some things a cat can do?

3. Which adaptations help a cat catch its prey?

4. How is a cat like its wild relatives? How is it different?

5. Can you name some words that describe a cat?

Cat Planning Sheet

Module: _____

Concepts: _____

_____

_____

_____

Vocabulary: _____

_____

_____

Questions to stimulate thought and discussion:

Remembering _____

_____

Understanding _____

_____

Applying _____

_____

Analyzing _____

_____

Evaluating _____

_____

Creating _____

_____

Cat Planning Sheet

Knowledge Objectives: _____

_____

_____

Skill Objectives: _____

_____

_____

Related Subjects: _____

_____

_____

Activities: _____

_____

_____

_____

Resources and Materials: _____

_____

_____

_____

Values and Attitudes: _____

_____

Evaluation: _____

_____

Deer

Animal Kingdom Planning Sheet

Animal of the month:

Deer

Month:

My Activities Plan

_____
_____
_____
_____
_____

Some things I want to know about:

Food

_____
_____

Habitat

_____
_____

Adaptations

_____
_____

10

The Deer Family Portrait

A male deer is called a _____.

A female deer is called a _____.

A baby deer is called a _____.

Habitat

The _____ is home to the deer.

Draw some things found in this habitat.
Draw the animal too.

Can you include other animals that might live here?

13

Camouflage
How a Deer Hides

Now you see me.

Draw the animal alone.

Now you don't.

Draw the animal in its habitat.

Animal Record Sheet

Animal's Name: Deer

Draw the animal.

Now label the animal's parts.

Record of important facts:

1. _____
2. _____
3. _____
4. _____
5. _____
6. _____

Special words: _____
_____

Animal's habitat: _____

15

Animal Facts: Deer

Passage to Read Aloud

The woods and forests of our country are home to many different kinds of animals. If you were to take a walk in the woods and stand quietly for a moment, you might hear a rustle of leaves and see a flash of white dart past. You probably glimpsed the white underside of a deer's tail. No doubt the deer caught your scent. When a deer is frightened, it holds its head up and sniffs, flips its tail up, and begins to run. Deer run so swiftly that they usually can get away from their enemies.

A baby deer is called a fawn and is born in the spring. It has a spotted coat that blends in with the leaves and twigs on the ground. The mother deer is called a doe, and the father deer is called a buck. In the winter, the buck and doe have gray or brown coats that blend with the dull winter forest. In warmer weather, their coats change to a reddish brown color. The buck is larger than the doe. He weighs about three hundred pounds and is five feet tall. The buck has antlers that he uses to ward off enemies. He sheds the antlers each winter, but they grow back each spring. At first the new antlers are knobby and covered with soft fur, but as they grow, they become strong and hard.

The deer family lives with other deer in a herd. Deer are known as herbivores. This means that they eat plants, such as leaves, berries, buds, and other vegetation that grow in their forest home. At first the fawn, like all baby mammals, drinks milk from its mother. Their forest home provides the deer with good water from streams and ponds.

A long time ago, deer were hunted by predators like wolves. When more and more people came to America, they didn't like the wolves eating their cows and sheep, so they killed most of the wolves. Without the wolves, the deer had no predators, so there was nothing to keep the deer population under control. Now there are millions of deer in the United States. If there are too many deer, there won't be enough food for them all, so the government allows people to hunt them to keep the population at a healthy number.

QUESTIONS:

1. Can you name each member of the deer family? What do they look like?
2. How does a fawn's spotted coat help it survive?
3. How does a deer's coat change with the seasons?
4. Why are there so many deer in the United States today?
5. Can you tell a short story about a deer?

Deer Planning Sheet

Module: _____

Concepts: _____

_____

_____

_____

Vocabulary: _____

_____

_____

Questions to stimulate thought and discussion:

Remembering _____

_____

Understanding _____

_____

Applying _____

_____

Analyzing _____

_____

Evaluating _____

_____

Creating _____

_____

Deer Planning Sheet

Knowledge Objectives: _____

_____

_____

Skill Objectives: _____

_____

_____

Related Subjects: _____

_____

_____

Activities: _____

_____

_____

_____

Resources and Materials: _____

_____

_____

_____

Values and Attitudes: _____

_____

Evaluation: _____

_____

Horse

16

Animal Kingdom Planning Sheet

Animal of the month:

Horse

Month:

My Activities Plan

_____
_____
_____
_____
_____

Some things I want to know about:

Food

_____
_____

Habitat

_____
_____

Adaptations

_____
_____

The Horse Family Portrait

A baby horse is called a _____.

18

Animal Record Sheet

Animal's Name: Horse

Draw the animal.

Now label the animal's parts.

Record of important facts:

1. _____
2. _____
3. _____
4. _____
5. _____
6. _____

Special words: _____

Animal's habitat: _____

19

Animal Facts: Horse

Passage to Read Aloud

There are many different kind of horses. Some horses are wild, but most horses are domesticated, which means that they have been tamed by people. Horses come in many shapes, sizes, and colors. Small horses are called ponies. Large, heavy, work horses are called draft horses.

Horses have long tails and manes. A horse's nose is called a muzzle. Their feet are called hooves. The hooves grow and need to be trimmed, just like our fingernails. When horses run, we say they are galloping. Male horses are called stallions or geldings, female horses are called mares, and babies are called foals. Foals have long wobbly legs and nurse from their mothers. Soon they are able to graze on grass. By the time they are two years old, they are about the same size as their parents.

Before cars were invented, people relied on horses for most of their transportation and work needs. Horses helped people by pulling wagons and sleds and by carrying heavy loads. They also carried soldiers into battle. For about a year and a half, horses were also used to carry the mail all across the United States. This was called the Pony Express.

Today horses are mostly used for pleasure. People like to ride them and compete in different kinds of sports with them, including horse racing. Some cowboys still use horses to round up the cattle on their ranches. Horses are also used by police officers in some cities to control crowds.

Most domesticated horses live in a barn or a stable. Inside the barn the horse lives in a stall. The fenced area around the outside of the stable is called the pasture. Some horses live in the pasture all the time and never live in a barn. As long as the horse has a place to go to get out of the rain and wind, most horses can live outdoors without any problems.

Horses eat grass, hay, and grain. A horse's saddle and other equipment are called tack. The horse's food, tack, bedding, and veterinary care can cost a lot of money, and it can take a lot of work to take care of a horse. However, most people who own horses enjoy them so much that they don't mind the hard work.

Have you ever gone horseback riding? Do you wish you could own a pony or a horse? Since a pony is smaller than a horse, most young riders start on a pony. Horses enjoy treats just like you do. They like apples, carrots, and peppermints. Horses are timid by nature, so always approach slowly and talk softly. If you keep calm, the horse will too. Be friendly, and the horse will usually respond in the same way.

QUESTIONS:

1. Can you describe a horse? Can you name its parts?
2. How have horses helped people throughout history?
3. Where do most horses live?
4. What do horses eat?
5. Would you like to have a horse? Why or why not?

Horse Planning Sheet

Module: _____

Concepts: _____

_____

_____

_____

Vocabulary: _____

_____

_____

Questions to stimulate thought and discussion:

Remembering _____

_____

Understanding _____

_____

Applying _____

_____

Analyzing _____

_____

Evaluating _____

_____

Creating _____

_____

Horse Planning Sheet

Knowledge Objectives: _____

_____

_____

Skill Objectives: _____

_____

_____

Related Subjects: _____

_____

_____

Activities: _____

_____

_____

_____

Resources and Materials: _____

_____

_____

_____

Values and Attitudes: _____

_____

Evaluation: _____

_____

Lion

Animal Kingdom Planning Sheet

Animal of the month:

Lion

Month:

My Activities Plan

_____
_____
_____
_____
_____

Some things I want to know about:

Food

_____
_____

Habitat

_____
_____

Adaptations

_____
_____

The Lion Family Portrait

A baby lion is called a _____.

Habitat

The _____ is home to the lion.

Draw some things found in this habitat.
Draw the animal too.

Can you include other animals that might live here?

23

Camouflage
How a Lion Hides

Now you see me.

Draw the animal alone.

Now you don't.

Draw the animal in its habitat.

Animal Record Sheet

Animal's Name: Lion

Draw the animal.

Now label the animal's parts.

Record of important facts:

1. _____
2. _____
3. _____
4. _____
5. _____
6. _____

Special words: _____
_____

Animal's habitat: _____

25

Animal Facts: Lion

Passage to Read Aloud

Do you know which animal is called the king of the beasts? If you said the lion, you're right. With his huge, shaggy mane, the male lion certainly looks impressive. Young males have a light-colored mane. Older males have a dark brown or black mane.

Lions have a tawny or golden brown coat with a dark tuft at the end of their tail. Grown males are about nine feet long and three feet high and may weigh up to four hundred pounds. Females are the same color but are smaller and do not have a mane.

If you were to take a trip to the grasslands of Africa, you would be able to see lions living in their natural habitat. You might even hear the lion's loud roar. Lions are the only member of the cat family to live in a group. The group is called a pride. Lions live, hunt, and play happily together.

Lions are carnivores, or meat eaters, and they hunt every three days or so. The females do most of the hunting. Lions hunt at night. They can see very well in the dark. This helps them as they prowl and hunt in the dark. Lions stalk the animals they want to catch. They hide near the water holes to wait for antelope, zebras, and other animals and then pounce on them. A lion can leap far, sometimes more than twenty feet. Lions are strong and can catch a much larger animal. They sleep a lot between hunting trips. Sometimes they sleep as much as twenty hours a day.

Baby lions are called cubs. There are usually four to six in a litter. They are small and blind when they are born. They are born in a bed of grass or thick brush or in a rocky cave. Cubs are as helpless as kittens. Cubs are about the size of a house cat when they are born. For the first weeks they have thick woolly coats that have stripes along the body and spots on the legs. Like other baby mammals, they drink milk from their mothers. They are frisky and romp and play just like kittens. When they are old enough, adult lions teach the lion cubs how to hunt and survive in the wild.

Young male lions do not grow manes until they are about three years old. Young lions are good at climbing trees until they are half grown.

Lions are related to house cats. Both lions and cats sleep a lot during the day and are active at night. Both of them are carnivores. Cats pounce on their prey in much the same way that lions do. However, lions do not make good pets!

QUESTIONS:

1. Where would you go to look for a lion?
2. Can you describe the lion family group and tell how they live?
3. What adaptations help a lion catch its prey?
4. How are lions and cats alike? How are they different?
5. Do you think a lion should be called the king of the beasts?

Lion Planning Sheet

Module: _____

Concepts: _____

_____

_____

_____

Vocabulary: _____

_____

_____

Questions to stimulate thought and discussion:

Remembering _____

_____

Understanding _____

_____

Applying _____

_____

Analyzing _____

_____

Evaluating _____

_____

Creating _____

_____

Lion Planning Sheet

Knowledge Objectives: _____

_____

_____

Skill Objectives: _____

_____

_____

Related Subjects: _____

_____

_____

Activities: _____

_____

_____

_____

Resources and Materials: _____

_____

_____

_____

Values and Attitudes: _____

_____

Evaluation: _____

_____

Elephant

26

Animal Kingdom Planning Sheet

Animal of the month:

Elephant

Month:

My Activities Plan

_____
_____
_____
_____
_____

Some things I want to know about:

Food

_____
_____

Habitat

_____
_____

Adaptations

_____

Habitat

The _____ is home to the elephant.

Draw some things found in this habitat.
Draw the animal too.

Can you include other animals that might live here?

28

Animal Record Sheet

Animal's Name: Elephant

Draw the animal.

Now label the animal's parts.

Record of important facts:

1. _____
2. _____
3. _____
4. _____
5. _____
6. _____

Special words: _____
_____

Animal's habitat: _____

29

Animal Facts: Elephant

Passage to Read Aloud

Have you ever gone to the zoo or a circus and been amazed at the size of those great animals called elephants? Elephants are mammals, and they are the largest land animals in the world. They can weigh up to six and a half tons. That's 13,000 pounds!

If you wanted to visit elephants in their natural habitat, you would have to go to the rain forests of Africa or India. The African elephant is bigger than the Indian elephant. The easiest way to tell the difference between African elephants and Indian elephants is by their ears. Indian elephants have small, triangular-shaped ears, while African elephants have large, fan-shaped ears. Another difference is the shape of the elephant's back. African elephants have a back that sags, while Indian elephants have an arched back.

If you were looking for elephants during the day, you'd find them near a cool and shady place by a river or a lake. You might hear the trumpeting call of the elephants. Elephants rest and sleep during the heat of the day. They sleep standing up. The elephant father is called a bull, the mother is a cow, and the baby is a calf. Elephants travel in groups of about fifty called herds. Elephants are herbivores and eat plants, roots, and berries. Because elephants are so large, they eat and drink a lot. Some eat almost six hundred pounds of food and drink fifty gallons of water each day. Would you like to do the grocery shopping for a family of elephants?

How do elephants get their food? They move quietly through the rain forest at night on their large, sturdy, cushioned feet. They pull up trees and eat leaves and berries as they go. A cow is usually the leader, and one by one the elephants follow her through the rain forest.

Do you wonder why elephants look so wrinkled? Did you think it is because they are old? Well, elephants do live to be very old—sometimes sixty or seventy years—but they are wrinkled for a different reason. All other mammals have a layer of fat under their skin to help insulate them from the cold. Elephants don't have this layer of fat, so their skin sags and looks wrinkled.

The elephant has the longest nose in the world, called a trunk. Elephants use their trunks for all sorts of things. They get a drink of water by sucking the water up with their trunks and squirting it into their mouths. They also squirt water over their backs to cool themselves off. Sometimes elephants use their trunks to spray themselves with sand to keep the bugs away. Elephants can also use their trunks to lift and pull things, much like people use their hands. Elephants' trunks are *prehensile*. This means the trunk can act like fingers to pick up even small objects. Have you ever seen an elephant pick up a peanut?

The elephant's tusks are two very large teeth which the elephant uses for carrying things, for protection, and for digging up trees. The tusks are made of ivory. Poachers hunt elephants illegally to get the ivory. Many elephants have been killed because people wanted to take their tusks to make jewelry and trinkets.

Today both African and Indian elephants are at risk of extinction. This means that there aren't very many of them, and if we are not careful, the last ones might die so that there will be no more of them in the world. This would be a terrible tragedy. We should do everything we can to protect elephants so that will never happen.

QUESTIONS:

1. Can you describe an elephant? Can you name its parts?

2. How can you tell the difference between an African elephant and an Indian elephant?

3. Where would you look for an elephant during the heat of the day?

4. How do the elephant's tusks help it survive?

5. Do you think there should be laws to protect wildlife?

Elephant Planning Sheet

Module: _____

Concepts: _____

_____

_____

_____

Vocabulary: _____

_____

_____

Questions to stimulate thought and discussion:

Remembering _____

_____

Understanding _____

_____

Applying _____

_____

Analyzing _____

_____

Evaluating _____

_____

Creating _____

_____

Elephant Planning Sheet

Knowledge Objectives: _____

_____

_____

Skill Objectives: _____

_____

_____

Related Subjects: _____

_____

_____

Activities: _____

_____

_____

_____

Resources and Materials: _____

_____

_____

_____

Values and Attitudes: _____

_____

Evaluation: _____

_____

Kangaroo

Animal Kingdom Planning Sheet

Animal of the month:

Kangaroo

Month:

My Activities Plan

_____
_____
_____
_____
_____

Some things I want to know about:

Food
_____
_____

Habitat
_____
_____

Adaptations
_____
_____

Habitat

The _____ is home to the kangaroo.

Draw some things found in this habitat.
Draw the animal too.

Can you include other animals that might live here?

Animal Record Sheet

Animal's Name: Kangaroo

Draw the animal.

Now label the animal's parts.

Record of important facts:

1. _____
2. _____
3. _____
4. _____
5. _____
6. _____

Special words: _____

_____

Animal's habitat: _____

Animal Facts: Kangaroo

Passage to Read Aloud

You'd have to travel a long way to visit the curious creature called the kangaroo. Kangaroos live all over Australia. These quiet, peaceable animals can be found in the dry plains of central Australia or the forests along the coast. The explorers who landed in Australia more than 350 years ago were certainly surprised when they first saw a kangaroo. It was different from any animal they knew.

Perhaps you've seen pictures of kangaroos. Maybe you've visited a zoo and have seen a live kangaroo. Kangaroos are the largest of the *marsupials*. All marsupials carry their young in pouches. The kangaroo's pouch is called a *marsupium*. It looks like a deep pocket built right into the front of her body. Baby kangaroos develop within this pouch. Kangaroos usually have only one baby at a time. The kangaroo baby is called a joey. It calls this cozy pouch home until it is able to care for itself. Baby kangaroos are very small when they are born. They are only one inch long, which is tiny for an animal that will grow taller than a man. When it is big enough, the kangaroo baby jumps out of the pouch. When danger comes or it is time to travel, it jumps right back in. The only thing sticking out as a joey rides along is its face. The mother and little joey squeak and cluck to each other to talk.

Kangaroos graze on green grass and plants. They are always on the move in search of new grass to eat and water to drink. Sometimes they graze side by side with cattle and sheep. When food is scarce or the water supply gets low, they move on. They often must travel far to find the food and water they need to stay alive.

Kangaroos travel in family groups called mobs. A mob usually has three females with joeys, a mature male kangaroo, and two or three young males. In places where food and water are plentiful, several family mobs graze together.

The most common kind of kangaroo is more than seven feet tall and has gray or reddish brown fur. A wallaby is a smaller-sized kangaroo. There is also the rat kangaroo, which is only a little more than a foot tall.

Most kangaroos live in the open grassy plains. Some live in trees, such as the smaller Black Tree Kangaroo. These animals have special non-skid pads on their feet and long claws to help them climb and keep them from falling.

The name kangaroo means "there he goes." This name is a good one because kangaroos move quickly. Kangaroos run from danger. Sometimes a male kangaroo uses its hind legs to kick while balancing on its tail. This is called boxing. The kangaroo's tail is a tool that helps it survive. Kangaroos use it for balance in running and jumping. They also use it as a seat while resting. With its long, strong tail and big hind feet, a kangaroo can leap as far as twenty-five feet with one hop. Most kangaroos can run faster than horses.

Even while resting, the kangaroo is alert to danger. Kangaroos sit with their body upright and their front legs off the ground. Their long pointed ears twitch on their dog-like heads. At the first sign of danger, a kangaroo thumps the ground hard with its big hind feet. Right away all the kangaroos start running. There he goes....

QUESTIONS:

1. Have you ever seen a kangaroo?

2. Why is a kangaroo called a marsupial?

3. How does a kangaroo's tail help it get away from danger?

4. Why might sheep ranchers not want a kangaroo on their land?

5. What is the most interesting fact you've learned about kangaroos?

Kangaroo Planning Sheet

Module: _____

Concepts: _____

_____

_____

_____

Vocabulary: _____

_____

_____

Questions to stimulate thought and discussion:

Remembering _____

_____

Understanding _____

_____

Applying _____

_____

Analyzing _____

_____

Evaluating _____

_____

Creating _____

_____

Kangaroo Planning Sheet

Knowledge Objectives: _____

_____

_____

Skill Objectives: _____

_____

_____

Related Subjects: _____

_____

_____

Activities: _____

_____

_____

_____

Resources and Materials: _____

_____

_____

_____

Values and Attitudes: _____

_____

Evaluation: _____

_____

Robin

34

Animal Kingdom Planning Sheet

Animal of the month:

Robin

Month:

My Activities Plan

_____
_____
_____
_____
_____

Some things I want to know about:

Food
_____
_____

Habitat
_____
_____

Adaptations
_____
_____

Habitat

The _____ is home to the robin.

Draw some things found in this habitat.
Draw the animal too.

Can you include other animals that might live here?

36

Animal Record Sheet

Animal's Name: Robin

Draw the animal.

Now label the animal's parts.

Record of important facts:

1. _____
2. _____
3. _____
4. _____
5. _____
6. _____

Special words: _____
_____

Animal's habitat: _____

37

Animal Facts: Robin

Passage to Read Aloud

Robins are known to many people as the first sign of spring. Their cheerful song and friendly ways are welcome after a long, cold winter. Robins are migratory birds. This means that they fly south for the winter and return in early spring. Robins are a member of the thrush family. They are gray with a bright red breast. They have long pointed wings and are strong fliers. Like all birds, robins have hollow bones that help to make them light enough to fly. Robins live in both rural and suburban areas and are a familiar sight to many people.

All kinds of animals have babies. Animal babies are born in different ways. Baby birds come from eggs laid by their mothers. The babies grow inside the eggs and then use their beaks to peck their way out of the egg. Birds build nests to lay their eggs in and take care of their young. Robins build their nests in trees. Sometimes they build them in bushes or shrubs. They may even build them under a roof or on a windowsill. Mother robin works very hard to build her nest. She makes many trips to and fro with twigs and grass. She adds a layer of mud to hold everything together. If she can't find mud, she makes some by putting dirt in her beak and dipping it in water. Then she lines the nest with soft grass and feathers. Her eggs are bluish-green, and she sits on them for about two weeks until they hatch. Father robin carefully guards this territory while mother robin hatches the eggs. He keeps his mate supplied with food while the eggs are incubated.

Baby robins need care. They are helpless and do not have any feathers. They cannot fly. They need to be fed. They keep opening their mouths and peeping for more food. Both the male and female robin fly back and forth many times during the day to feed their hungry brood. The robins' favorite food is earthworms, but they eat insects too. Robins also eat berries and similar fruits.

As baby robins get older, they are taught to keep themselves neat and clean. This is called preening. Feathers that are smooth and sleek help a bird fly well. They keep their feet clean by picking at them with their bills. They scrape their bills against tree branches to clean them.

Keep your eyes open this spring to see if you can sight the first robin.

QUESTIONS:

1. How is the way baby birds come into this world different from other animals?
2. Why do robins fly south for the winter?
3. What adaptations help a bird fly well?
4. Can you describe a robin's nest?
5. Can you make up a poem about a robin?

Robin Planning Sheet

Module: _____

Concepts: _____

_____

_____

_____

Vocabulary: _____

_____

_____

Questions to stimulate thought and discussion:

Remembering _____

_____

Understanding _____

_____

Applying _____

_____

Analyzing _____

_____

Evaluating _____

_____

Creating _____

_____

Robin Planning Sheet

Knowledge Objectives: _____

_____

_____

Skill Objectives: _____

_____

_____

Related Subjects: _____

_____

_____

Activities: _____

_____

_____

_____

Resources and Materials: _____

_____

_____

_____

Values and Attitudes: _____

_____

Evaluation: _____

_____

Ladybug

38

Animal Kingdom Planning Sheet

Animal of the month:

Ladybug

Month:

My Activities Plan

_____
_____
_____
_____
_____

Some things I want to know about:

Food

_____
_____

Habitat

_____
_____

Adaptations

_____
_____

39

Habitat

The _____ is home to the ladybug.

Draw some things found in this habitat.
Draw the animal too.

Can you include other animals that might live here?

40

Animal Record Sheet

Animal's Name: Ladybug

Draw the animal.

Now label the animal's parts.

Record of important facts:

1. _____
2. _____
3. _____
4. _____
5. _____
6. _____

Special words: _____
_____

Animal's habitat: _____

41

49

Animal Facts: Ladybug

Passage to Read Aloud

There are many different kinds of insects. How many insects can you name?

Ladybugs are small spotted insects. Spiders and bees are insects too. The ladybug is a type of beetle. It is actually called a Ladybird Beetle, but almost everyone calls it a ladybug. Some insects like mosquitoes are harmful. Ladybugs are helpful insects, though. They are among our best insect friends. You have probably seen ladybugs before. They are easy to spot because they are brightly colored. The kind you saw was probably bright red with black spots. Not all ladybugs are this color. Some are yellow, and their spots can be black, red, white, or yellow. Ladybugs are tiny.

Ladybugs are helpful because they eat other insects that are harmful. The harmful insects they eat are called aphids. Aphids eat fruit on trees and suck the juice out. Many years ago the aphids started destroying all the oranges and lemons in some parts of the country. Back then we didn't have any ladybugs in this country, but some were brought in from another country, Australia. Soon the ladybugs stopped the aphids from destroying all the orange trees. So when you drink orange juice and enjoy it, you have the ladybug to thank.

The ladybug is like most other insects. It has six legs, as do all insects. It has a head with antennae and a mouth. The antennae are special aids to tell the ladybug what is happening around it. The head is connected to the ladybug's thorax—the part of the body to which all the legs and wings are attached. The thorax is attached to the abdomen. The ladybug breathes through tiny openings in the abdomen. This is very different from the way people breathe. Insects have wings, but ladybugs and other beetles are different from most insects because ladybugs have two sets of wings: a fragile inner set used for flying, and a tough, hard, outer set that protects the inner one.

Ladybugs lay clusters of bright yellow eggs on a leaf. These hatch into larval ladybugs, which gobble up aphids. The larvae do not look like ladybugs but instead are long, thin, and gray. Soon the larvae change into fat, round pupae. After six days or so, the skin of the pupae splits down the back, and out comes a full-grown ladybug.

In the winter ladybugs huddle together in a sheltered spot and sleep. People hunt these masses of ladybugs and put them in sacks with straw. They store them in a cool place. In the spring they sell them to farmers. The busy little ladybugs get right to work eating all the aphids to keep them from destroying the crops.

QUESTIONS:

1. Describe a ladybug. Can you name its parts?
2. How does a ladybug help farmers?
3. How does a ladybug's antennae help it survive?
4. How is a ladybug like a bee? How is it different?
5. Which insect do you think is most helpful to people?

Ladybug Planning Sheet

Module: _____

Concepts: _____

_____

_____

_____

Vocabulary: _____

_____

_____

Questions to stimulate thought and discussion:

Remembering _____

_____

Understanding _____

_____

Applying _____

_____

Analyzing _____

_____

Evaluating _____

_____

Creating _____

_____

Ladybug Planning Sheet

Knowledge Objectives: _____

_____

_____

Skill Objectives: _____

_____

_____

Related Subjects: _____

_____

_____

Activities: _____

_____

_____

_____

Resources and Materials: _____

_____

_____

_____

Values and Attitudes: _____

_____

Evaluation: _____

_____

Turtle

Animal Kingdom Planning Sheet

Animal of the month:

Turtle

Month:

My Activities Plan

_____

_____

_____

_____

_____

Some things I want to know about:

Food

_____

_____

Habitat

_____

_____

Adaptations

_____

_____

Habitat

The _____ is home to the turtle.

Draw some things found in this habitat.
Draw the animal too.

Can you include other animals that might live here?

Life Cycle

How a Turtle Grows and Changes

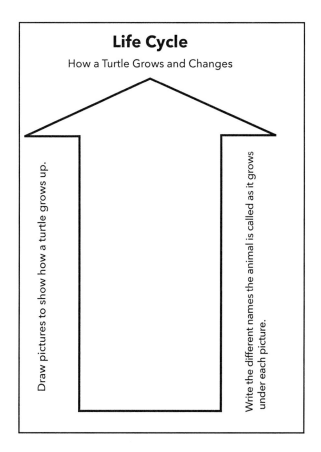

Draw pictures to show how a turtle grows up.

Write the different names the animal is called as it grows under each picture.

Animal Record Sheet

Animal's Name: Turtle

Draw the animal.

Now label the animal's parts.

Record of important facts:

1. _____

2. _____

3. _____

4. _____

5. _____

6. _____

Special words: _____

_____

Animal's habitat: _____

Animal Facts: Turtle

Passage to Read Aloud

There is an animal that carries its house wherever it goes. Can you guess who? If you said a turtle, you're right. Can you name another animal that carries its house around?

There was a time when most of the animals on the earth were reptiles. One of the oldest types of reptiles still living today is the turtle. This hardy creature has been around for almost two hundred million years. Some other reptiles are snakes and lizards.

Turtles, like all reptiles, are cold-blooded, which means they cannot keep themselves warm; their body temperature is the same as the temperature of their surroundings. When it is warm, they are more active. When it is cooler, they are sluggish. When it gets too cold, turtles hibernate in the ground or in the mud at the bottom of a stream or pond.

Turtles are omnivores, which means they eat both animals and plants. Turtles do not have teeth, but they have jaws with sharp edges that help them tear their food into little pieces. Because turtles do not burn calories to keep themselves warm, they can go for months without eating.

What makes turtles different from other reptiles is their strong shell. The shell is made of bone. The top portion is called the *carapice*, and the bottom or underside is called the *plastron*. The turtle's shell protects it from its enemies. The turtle is too slow to escape from them by running away. To escape harm, the turtle pulls its neck and limbs inside the protective shell. Turtles cannot travel quickly, so they have long necks to help them in searching for food and looking out for enemies. They can stretch their necks and turn them in all directions. Some turtles have webbed feet to help them travel more quickly in water.

Some kinds of turtles can live up to sixty years. Only a few kinds of turtles live on land. Turtles that live just on land are called tortoises. Most turtles live in fresh water, but the largest turtles live in the ocean. All turtles come ashore and lay their eggs in nests on land. Turtles do not stay around to hatch their eggs. Baby turtles have a special tooth that grows on the tip of their nose. They use this tooth to break out of their shell when it is time to hatch.

QUESTIONS:

1. Can you describe a turtle? Can you name its parts?
2. Why is a turtle a reptile?
3. What does a turtle eat?
4. What adaptations help a turtle protect itself?
5. Where do turtles live?

Turtle Planning Sheet

Module: _____

Concepts: _____

_____

_____

_____

Vocabulary: _____

_____

_____

Questions to stimulate thought and discussion:

Remembering _____

_____

Understanding _____

_____

Applying _____

_____

Analyzing _____

_____

Evaluating _____

_____

Creating _____

_____

Turtle Planning Sheet

Knowledge Objectives: _____

_____

_____

Skill Objectives: _____

_____

_____

Related Subjects: _____

_____

_____

Activities: _____

_____

_____

_____

Resources and Materials: _____

_____

_____

_____

Values and Attitudes: _____

_____

Evaluation: _____

_____

Chapter Three

Designing a Differentiated Curriculum

Developing Creativity

The right classroom conditions can allow creativity to flourish in children. Not all children are creative, but teachers can do much to encourage the development of creative behaviors by employing certain methods and strategies, such as:

- Brainstorming

- Problem-solving activities

- Open-ended questions

- Divergent/productive thinking tasks

Teachers should incorporate activities that elicit creative responses into their lesson plans. For example, they can encourage children to develop traits of spontaneity and resourcefulness by encouraging independent work and original products. A warm and accepting classroom atmosphere supports initiative and creative expression.

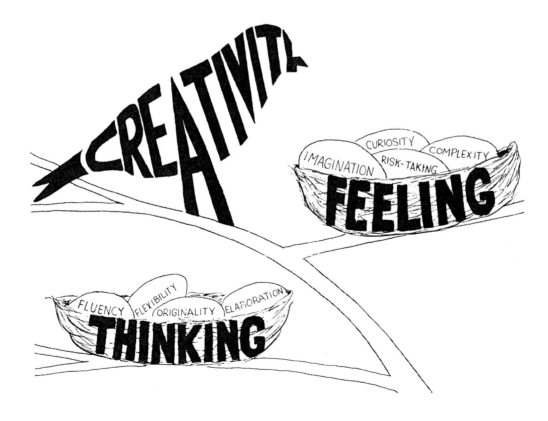

Creative Behaviors

COGNITIVE – THINKING	AFFECTIVE – FEELING
Fluency (quantity of ideas) Generating a number of relevant responses	**Risk Taking (courage)** Tolerance for ambiguity, taking a chance, presenting and defending ideas
Flexibility (number of categories) Generating a variety of classes, ideas, and approaches	**Complexity (challenge)** Pursuing difficult tasks, seeking alternative actions, organizing
Originality (number of new ideas) Generating novel uses; unique solutions; clever, subtle, or unusual responses	**Curiosity (inquisitiveness)** Pursuing, discovering, exploring, reflective thinking, following up on hunches
Elaboration (expanding or adapting previous ideas) Giving details, expanding basic concepts or ideas	**Imagination (intuition)** Daydreaming, fantasizing, feeling intuitively, pretending, wondering

The following ideas are examples of ways to develop creativity in young children.

Fluency

How many ways do birds help us? (Tell; make a list or chart; draw a picture or mural.)

Flexibility

Can you rearrange the letters in these scrambled words to make the names of some birds you know? (What else can you do with the words? Make a puzzle or riddle; form a design.)

Originality

Finish this sentence: "The little bird looked into my window and...." (Tell or write a story; plan a puppet show.)

Elaboration

Give this bird some feathers. (Use paints, string art, pine cones, or other art media.) Design a home for your bird.

Risk Taking

How would you help a bird that fell from its nest? (Plan a skit or role play; include the mother bird's reaction.)

Complexity

Make a new bird from parts of other birds. (Use cut-up coloring books or magazine pictures; design your own; use art materials.) Name your bird.

Curiosity

How do birds learn to fly? How do they learn to make nests? Where can you learn about birds? (Use books and other resources to plan a research project.)

Imagination

What would happen if you climbed into a big bird's nest? (Plan a skit or pantomime; write a story.)

Developing Higher-Order Thinking Skills

Educators agree that the best way to engage children in learning—and prepare them for life beyond school—is to help them develop higher-order thinking skills. Good questions asked by teachers lead to good thinking experiences and answers. An atmosphere of acceptance and openness to ideas leads to student confidence and exciting learning experiences.

A good way to help children move from lower-order thinking to higher-order thinking is through the use of Benjamin Bloom's *Taxonomy of Educational Objectives*, a classification that presents six major cognitive operations, which has been revised to include the following processes: remembering, understanding, applying, analyzing, evaluating, and creating. Remembering calls upon recall or memory of material as it was presented. Understanding calls upon memory of the material plus interpretation of its meaning. Applying calls upon using the learned material in a new situation. Analyzing calls upon examining and breaking the learned material into its distinguishable parts and the ability to explore their relationships. Evaluating calls upon being judgmental using criteria and standards. Creating calls upon planning and reorganizing known elements into something new in form or evolving a completely new idea.

Teachers can plan questions and learning experiences for all the children in their classroom by using the different thinking levels.

A Chart Based on

Bloom's Taxonomy of the Cognitive Domain

Different Levels of Thinking

CLASSIFICATION	TYPES OF QUESTIONS	STUDENT ACTIVITIES
Remembering	Can you tell, list, recognize, describe, define, relate who, what, where, when, why?	Gather data, memorize, name, observe, show, record, locate
Understanding	Can you tell in your own words, interpret, explain, summarize?	Classify, demonstrate, group, illustrate, rearrange, reorder
Applying	Can you use the information, problem-solve?	Model, order, use acquired data in new learning situations, operate
Analyzing	What are the causes, consequences, steps of process? Can you arrange, examine?	Compare, contrast, take apart, dissect, investigate, discuss
Evaluating	Can you set standards, judge, choose, decide?	Criticize, justify choices and actions, decide according to a standard, prove
Creating	Can you think of different ways, how else, design, improve, develop?	Imagine, predict, design, improve, change, invent, adapt

Bloom's Taxonomy Applied

What about animals?

Creating

I can use these art supplies to make a puppet of an imaginary animal.

Evaluating

I don't think it would be a good idea to keep a robin in a birdcage because robins need room to fly.

Analyzing

Cats and lions are the same in many ways, but they are also different in some important ways.

Understanding

All mammals need air, whether they live on land or in the water.

Applying

I think the new animal in our science corner is a mammal because it is furry, and it is feeding its baby milk from its body.

Remembering

Baby whales are called calves, and their mothers are called cows.

Bloom's Taxonomy Activities

Remembering

- Gather data
- Record
- Relate

Pick an animal. Find out all the facts you can about this animal. Observe the animal (film, zoo, etc.). Read books. Ask questions. Listen to people. Make a list of facts and vocabulary words about this animal.

Look at a picture of an animal, or draw a picture of an animal. Name or label its parts.

Make a puppet of an animal. Let the puppet tell what it eats, where it lives, and how it gets away from danger.

Make a dictionary about animals. Write an animal's name on an index card. Write facts about the animal on the back. Do this for several animals. Then alphabetize the cards. Punch holes in the cards, and tie them all together with yarn.

Understanding

- Illustrate
- Describe
- Recall

Draw a picture of an animal. Discuss how the animal moves. Use words to describe the animal's movements, either by saying them or by writing them. Examples:

whale – glides	elephant – lumbers
cat – crouches	kangaroo – bounds
deer – leaps	robin – soars
horse – gallops	ladybug – flits
lion – pounces	turtle – crawls

Each animal has its own pattern of movement. Can you imitate the movements of the different animals?

Applying

- Use data
- Apply data
- Demonstrate

What does *hibernate* mean? Make a list of animals that use this adaptation to survive. Choose one of the animals. Fold a piece of drawing paper in half. Draw a picture of this animal in its summer home on one half and a picture of the animal in its winter home on the other half.

If an animal that usually hibernates in the winter does not hibernate when it gets cold, what problems would it have?

How does camouflage help an animal? Make a list of animals that use this adaptation to survive. Choose one of the animals. Draw a picture of this animal. Now draw the animal's environment in the picture. Is it still easy to see the animal?

Make a list of animals that use camouflage to survive. Are there some animals that need to hide more than others (big/small, predator/prey)?

Build or buy a bird feeder. Put seeds or suet out. Observe birds at the feeder. What birds come? How do they behave? Draw a picture of what you see.

Relate and apply concepts by working on other projects, such as an ant farm or a terrarium.

Analyzing

- Investigate
- Compare
- Classify

Choose two animals. How are these animals alike? How are they different?

Make animal silhouettes out of colored construction paper. Cut out animals, various animal parts (sets of ears, etc.), and related environmental objects (plants, etc.). Use these to associate a trait with an animal, to group animals, or to contrast environments. Investigate life cycles, life spans, and adaptations to the environment. Discuss ways to classify animals (food, habitat, shape, etc.). Make a mural, chart, or graph. For example:

Ears	Legs	Feet	Coverings	Foods	Habitats
Cat	6 – Insects	Webbed	Hide	Omnivores	Forest
Asian Elephant	4 – Most mammals	Cushioned	Fur	Herbivores	Plains
African Elephant	2 – Birds, people	Hooves	Feathers	Carnivores	Jungle
Horse	0 – Whales (flippers)	Claws	Shell		Ocean
Deer		Talons	Skin		
Whale					
Turtle					
Bird					
Insect (antennae)					

How do adaptations protect animals? Make a chart. List animal names, name a part of each animal, and tell how these structures help the animal survive. For example:

Survival Chart

Animal	Part	Use
cat	claws	hold its prey
elephant	tusks	uproot trees
fawn	spotted coat	hide from enemies

Evaluating

- Decide
- Choose
- Prove

Use questions to stimulate children's thinking. Invite their comments, questions, and reactions. Guide them in justifying their choices. Help them establish criteria for their decisions.

Are robins and ladybugs useful animals? How are they useful? Which would you most like to discover in your backyard? Why?

Which animal would be most easily trained: a pony, a cat, a lion, or an elephant? Why?

Would you want to train this animal? What would you have it do?

Are wild animals better off living in their natural habitat or in the zoo? Does this go for all wild animals? Give reasons for your decisions.

Should there be laws to protect endangered species?

If you were a veterinarian, would you choose to care for pets, farm animals, or zoo animals? Why? Which would be easiest to care for? Which group of animals would be the most interesting to care for?

Make a mural of the animals that you think are the most helpful to people. Show ways they are useful.

Survey your classmates. Find out which animal is their favorite. Make a graph of the responses.

What do you think is the most interesting thing about each animal you've studied? Draw a picture of each animal, and write a sentence about the most interesting fact. Put your pictures together to make a book of animal facts.

Creating

- Imagine
- Design
- Adapt

Imagine that you could change into a whale or a cat. Which one would you choose to be? What adventure might you have? Write a story. Draw a picture for your story.

Make a puppet that looks like an animal. Plan a play to tell the animal's story.

Make an animal model:

Ladybug – Paint a smooth, flat rock.
Robin – Draw and color a paper cutout, or make a mobile.
Lion – Make a mask, or plan a skit.
Horse – Make a duo-fold stand-up cutout.
Turtle – Use a paper plate or walnut shell.

Design a diorama of a kangaroo's habitat. Show a mother kangaroo and her joey.

Create a mural showing deer in their habitat. How many other animals found in the same habitat can you include?

Make a set of animal riddle cards. Write the animal's name on one side of the card and the riddle on the other. Examples:

I carry my house around. (Turtle)
I never need a babysitter. (Kangaroo)

How many different riddles can you think of for each animal? Ask a friend to help you.

Worksheets

The worksheets in the student book are designed to enable children to gather and apply information, practice skills, and expand concepts in creative and innovative ways. The activities encourage problem-solving behaviors as the children engage in application, analysis, and evaluation. A planning worksheet is included for each animal to help children develop skills of self-management and self-direction. The rest of the worksheets follow Bloom's Taxonomy:

Remembering	Animal Record Sheet
Understanding	The Family Portrait Habitat
Applying	Camouflage
Analyzing	Life Cycle Life Span Adaptation What Do Animals Eat?
Evaluating	My Favorite Animal
Creating	Imagine You Are an Animal A Model Elephant

Life Span

Make a graph. Compare how long each animal lives.
Use a different color for each animal.

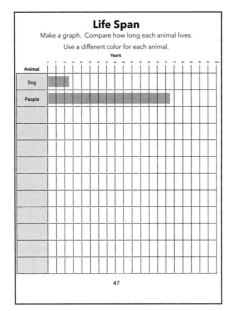

Adaptation

Animal Survival Chart

Animal	Part	Use
Giraffe	Long neck	Reaches leaves to eat

48

My Favorite Animal

My favorite animal is the _____.

I like the _____ best because _____
_____

Some good words to describe my favorite animal are:
_____
_____

The most interesting thing a _____ can do is
_____

Some important things in my favorite animal's habitat are:
_____

I would like to visit my favorite animal at its home in the:
_____

49

What Do Animals Eat?

Directions: Write each animal's name in an oval. Then color the ovals to show what each animal eats.

Colors: Plant eaters – Green
          Meat eaters – Red
          Plant and meat eaters – Blue

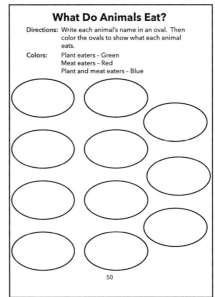

50

Imagine You Are an Animal #1

If I could be a _____,
how would my life be different?
  • How would I look?
  • Where would I live?
  • What things could I do?

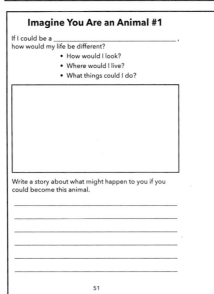

Write a story about what might happen to you if you could become this animal.

_____
_____
_____
_____
_____

51

A Model Elephant

Cut out the model. Stand your elephant up.
How does the model compare with the real animal?

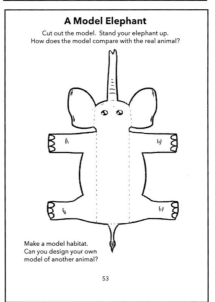

Make a model habitat.
Can you design your own model of another animal?

53

66